I0176587

The
25
Indisputable
Laws
of
Style

Sean Coyle

Solomon Publishing & Consulting Group
First printing September 1, 2015

ISBN:978-0-9966826-3-3

A big thank you to Matthew Conway for his advice and help on this project.

Sean Coyle

FOR MY WIFE & SON

A loving father and husband teaching his son how to develop self-confidence through example. It is my hope that he begins to understand how he can achieve anything he puts his mind, heart, and dedication of effort to.

You are what you make of yourself and you can make yourself anything you desire.

To Brock, a fine boy with incredible talents, and to Roxanne, this book is dedicated.

Contents

Preface

Why this book? Well the time is right. The spawn and sprawl of social media has exponentially sped up the personal and professional image-marketing machine. It has been happening at such a rapid pace that many cannot keep up. The world market is image- and style- focused now more than ever.

For several decades I have been tracking and studying trends for multiple apparel companies. I did this with the explicit goal of distilling the specific colors, products, fabrics, and styles the population would want now, and a year from now. The more researched, the more I saw how image and style shaped consumer demand.

Over time I noticed the impact that look and style had on different audiences. I also noticed the impact that style had on one's own mind and attitude.

People that showcased style seemed to be getting ahead while those who only offered substance never made it past the first pitch meeting. As a student of life and trends it is impossible not to learn the nature of people. In knowing the nature of people, one can make an educated guess about where they will spend their dollars. I have been doing this successfully for years.

My research and intuition led to a vision for a book on style and design. As I began writing the book I noticed that people cared less for the technical knowledge that I was sharing and more for image and style. I decided to list the 25 indisputable laws of style as guiding principles.

If you are crafting a style it is best to start with the laws and then dig deeper. This will help you map out the territory before picking your trail. Start now! Study the laws, know them, and utilize them to further your studies on style. Use them as a guide on how to craft your own style. Create and craft a vision for the best "you" that you can be. This is what the 25 indisputable laws of style are all about.

THE

25

INDISPUTABLE

LAWS

OF

STYLE

#1

The First Law

"Your clothing is a reflection of your desires"

I care about style and I want to be surrounded by like-minded people.

That is the message you are sending. If you want others to dress great all the time then you have to as well. You are creating and crafting your personal style because style matters to you. You have to put forth an effort, always. Having a definitive style is a decision you make. It is something that you do when no one is watching, and when you are out on the street. Make the effort. Throw out the underwear with holes in them and the shirts with small stains on them. If you think no one notices, you are wrong. Your choice of clothing is a direct reflection of your desires.

Style begins at home.

If you want to establish style then you need to exude it wherever and in whatever you are doing. There is appropriate attire for every situation. Go the extra mile and be a reflection of your expectations. Establishing your style and expectations will help you communicate your desires better. It will improve your confidence and help you develop a comfort in your style. If you have taken to wearing yoga pants and you don't work out, it speaks volumes about your personal expectations. You are sending a clear message—but not likely the one you want to send.

Having a definitive style is a decision you make.

It is something that you do when no one is watching as well as when you are out on the town. One of the easiest ways to think about this is to imagine what you want others to look like and the people you want to surround yourself with. Imagine what that looks like. Now place those same expectations on yourself.

Draw from your reservoir of images that you desire and then be those images in reverse. You have to make an effort. If you want the style of a successful stockbroker who wears two thousand dollar suits, you have to start becoming that image even if you don't have a stockbroker's bank account. Make a list of the looks you like. Pinterest is a great place to find images and pull together the looks that reflect the style you desire. Make the decision to be prepared. Know what you want. Do the research and gain the knowledge to make it happen when the time comes.

If you think no one notices, you are wrong. People might not tell you when your style is off. They just judge you, catalog who you are, and move on. You made an impression. Make sure the impression is one you want others to have of you—as well as the impression you want to have of you. When you look in the mirror, make sure you see all that is being conveyed by your image. Ask yourself "How does this make me look?" "What am I saying about myself?" "Does it reflect my own positive image of myself?

Who you are and the style you want to exude are written in the clothes you wear.

As well as how you wear them. The human race is hard-wired to categorize you and judge you so they can know how to treat you. How you want to be treated is determined by the visual messages you send. This includes what you will, and will not accept. Have high standards and you will be surprised by how many people will try to live up to them.

The 25 Indisputable Laws of Style

#2

The Second Law

"If you wouldn't wrap your baby in it, don't put yourself in it"

Fibers, yarns, and fabrics make a big difference.

Natural fibers are superior above all. They are natural. Man-made fibers can be great for some things, but if you would not wrap a newborn infant in the fabric, then shy away from it for yourself. Natural fabrics have inherent performance features to them. The addition of some man-made fabrics can enhance your experience depending on the item and end use. The price of the best natural and man-made fabrics vary with the market.

Great fabric starts with great fibers.

Great fibers come from the earth. Cotton, wool, silk, and linen are all great natural fibers. Man-made fibers can be engineered to have some wonderful properties; however my body has always told me it liked natural fibers best by a long shot. Cotton is hydrophilic, meaning it likes water. It is attracted to water and absorbs water. Think about this. The average adult foot sweats an 8 oz. glass of water in a day. My foot has told me that it feels better in cotton than other man made materials.

Man made materials come from a variety of chemicals.

They are mixed in a recipe and poured through a spinnerette to extrude fibers like nylon, polyester, and acetate, to name a few. These fibers can be engineered to have some performance. Be careful because companies often overstate and under deliver these performance characteristics. There are many that can add a true "extra experience" in your fabric. Lycra and stretch is one. Man-made fabrics are hydrophobic. They don't like water, but boy do they love oil. They tend to stain easy and hold in body odor, even after being washed, as the fiber opens to heat and closes when you wash it.

Why would you accept less than what you would give to a newborn infant?

For choosing everyday clothing, natural fibers are best. We wrap babies in soft cotton that breathes and prevents the baby's skin from having a negative reaction. It is important that you select the best for yourself as you build your style. It will help you feel good about your purchases.

When selecting the best fabrications, price will play a factor.

Because natural fibers and fabrics are subject to nature, their price goes up and down with the crops and yield. Bad weather can result in a small cotton crop and so the price of cotton will go up. Look for the best natural materials; such as long staple cotton fiber, Egyptian cotton, Pima cottons, Merino wools, and high momme silks. It will be worth the money and your body will thank you.

3

The Third Law

"If you are uncomfortable it does not fit"

How you feel has an affect on how you look.

If you are uncomfortable, you will not look your best or present yourself in the best light. You can be uncomfortable because your clothes do not fit well or because they do not fit who you are. Your clothes should never fit you like an over-stuffed sausage or a billowing sail. Be sure to present your best self and not a poor imitation of someone else. Being comfortable begins with your skin and continues with your clothes. Comfort frees your mind to focus on the tasks at hand.

When you are wearing clothing that fits great, it speaks for you.

You will feel better and will not be constantly adjusting to get comfortable. A man or a woman in a well-tailored suit has the look of power. Is there any item of clothing that does not look its best when the fit is perfect? It is worth spending the time, effort, and money to have clothes that fit like they were made for you and maybe they will be.

You look and feel better when clothes fit properly.

You can't fit ten pounds into a five-pound bag. Many have tried and many are trying. Please don't. If the items are too tight, they not only pull and gape, but also put others in fear of losing an eye if one of the buttons breaks loose of their holding. Today a lot of clothes are made using stretch. This can be woven, knit or spun into the yarns and fabrics. It is added to accentuate a fit, not to enable one to squeeze more into less. It can be eye opening when you realize your true size and not the vanity sizing you may have gotten use to. It is part of owning your style. Know your true size and work with it—not against it.

Being comfortable with your style and having clothes that fit comfortably will provide you with a degree of elegance.

Looking terrific and making it look so easy has a level of grace to it. You will be focused on the project, presentation, interview, or date, and your audience will be completely enamored with the ease in which you move and exist.

When crafting your style be sure that you are comfortable.

That may take practice. There is plenty of advice regarding fashion and style. Both evolve but style should grow. You should no more be a prisoner to your pants than you should be to a specific pattern. There is a reason tailors exist. Most off the rack clothes are meant to fit a range and not a specific person. Invest in a good tailor and enjoy the carefree feeling of great fitting clothes.

4

The Fourth Law

"You are judged by how you look"

First impressions are largely based on how you look and present yourself.

What is it that you would like your appearance to say about you? Take a look at some of the visual clues you are currently presenting. Ask yourself, "What are they saying about me?" It is important to remember that first impressions are probably not whom you really are deep down inside. However they are lasting. First impressions will linger and can be very difficult to change once cast.

So what is your style and look broadcasting about you?

More than ninety percent of communication comes from your body language. Less than ten percent is what comes out of your mouth. How you present yourself, your image, is the basis by which you are viewed. It is a lasting impression. Now imagine how much stronger your appearance is speaking during a first impression. Get out of your head and look in the mirror. Do some research on what images might project the message you want to broadcast?

What do you want your appearance and mannerisms to say about you?

Impressions and judgments are made very quickly. Humans are hard wired to do this easily and with only the information you provide. The mind will cross-reference your image with their experience to produce a first impression. That impression can be stored in the brain for a long time and will prove very difficult to alter.

What visual clues are you providing, and what are they saying about you?

Sloppy attire and unkempt hair, an unshaven face or legs, ill-fitting clothes, and scuffed shoes all send a specific message. Smart shoes, comfortable shoes, and sexy shoes all are sending a different message. Are you showing a lot of cleavage? Are you looking down your nose and across your high collar? Do you have a neck tattoo and full sleeves? There is no right nor wrong thing for style. You should have a very good understanding of what your image is saying. Know what impression it is leaving. Is your message fierce or friendly, dangerous or safe, attractive or homely, intelligent or dull? Or worse yet, is your message just plain uninteresting?

Impressions may be superficial, but they endure.

Sorry, but this is an indisputable fact, so ignore it at your own peril. Take the time and effort to ensure that the message you craft and send is aligned with how you see yourself. Dress how you want to be addressed. Remember that first impressions last.

5

The Fifth Law

"When you look good, you feel good"

There is a correlation between looking good and feeling good.

As you move through your environment, people reflect you back to you. When you look great and pulled together, that is what comes back to you. It is a self-fulfilling prophecy. You look great; you feel great; you perform great. This even holds true when you are not feeling great. Being pulled together with great style can change your life.

The world is a mirror held up to us.

We walk through life having an effect on everyone with whom we come in contact. The reaction that they send back to us has an immediate effect on how we feel. Have you ever walked through the airport and you pass a stunning person who has such style and elegance that you just want to stop and watch? You want to see this being that exists on another level. That is reflected back to that person and it makes their personal style that much more interesting. What a compliment. You get back what you send out.

Looking great can have an enormous effect on your performance.

When you are presenting, interviewing, or making a sales call; looking your best is a smart choice. When you look good, you feel like you own the moment. You tend to do your best when you are in sync and firing on all cylinders. You look good. You feel good. You are smiling and doing your work well. It produces positive, memorable results.

Even a great sports car with a little wear on it is still a great sports car.

Even if you aren't feeling particularly well, you will feel better if you look good. You feel better about yourself, and more confident. The mind will adapt to its surroundings. If you are part of the picture, looking great helps the mind reinforce good feelings.

Being well put together attracts good qualities to your persona.

Looking good is like having your happy dance on. When you feel so good you just want to dance. You're having a great time and you're a pleasure to be around. It has a certain magnetic quality about it.

6

The Sixth Law

"Price does not always equal quality"

It is best to search for value and not price.

Price can be deceptive and not always a guarantee of the best quality. Ask yourself, "Why is this expensive or not?" If all things are equal, then always buy the best in class. Constantly look for signs of quality in whatever you are purchasing.

Why search for value over price?

Well, a good pair of shoes may carry a more expensive price tag, but the better shoe may outlast the cheap shoe by years. On the other hand, if you are purchasing your high-ticket apparel items at an outlet store because of the label, you should know most companies' manufacture cheaper quality for their outlet stores. You are not getting a bargain if you are paying a lot for a cheaper quality.

It is important to understand the "why" behind a high price and a low price.

Is it a limited edition or a short production run? Is it special and a one of a kind? Some items may have a high price tag because they are in short supply, not because they are better quality. Many fashionistas want to be first. They want to be trend setters. Sometimes it costs more to be first because of inefficiencies in manufacturing. On the other hand, that great price may just exist because no one wants that item. Maybe the item is of poor quality. There is always the very real possibility that it is cheap because no one cared about how it was made. Who made it? How much did he or she suffer so you could have it cheap?

If all things are equal, and even if they aren't, buy best-in-class products.

Best-in-class products are those that made the brand you are purchasing famous. Ferragamo is famous for shoes and Burberry is famous for trench coats. A company will spend more time and effort, and have much more expertise on their signature products. They are company icons and have a far greater chance of being an exceptional value for the price.

Before purchasing you should make yourself familiar with signs of quality.
This should be for all of the products you intend to purchase. An educated consumer is much more likely to find value at any price. It helps you know when something is truly a deal. If you know best-in-class products, you can always add the ones you don't have to your wardrobe when they are priced right.

7

The Seventh Law

"Not all colors work for everyone"

It is amazing how many people never give any thought to what colors work well with their complexions and which don't.

There are several schools of thought on how to determine what skin tone or season you are. It doesn't matter which method you choose to use. Just follow a few simple common sense rules and you will be on your way to maximizing your style color sense.

It is important to get into a color comfort zone so you can maximize wardrobe impact.

Many people never consider why some colors work for them and others don't. Often if someone pays a compliment on a particular color you are wearing, the research stops there and that becomes a go-to color. Broaden your color horizons and the sky just may be the limit.

There are several methods most commonly used to determine your skin tone.

There is the season method where you determine if you are a winter/summer (cool tones) or a spring/fall (warm tones). There are also methods to just determine if you are pale, olive, or dark skin toned. All the methods break down into three major categories. Cool tone or paler/fairer skin; warm tones or olive and yellow skin tones; and darker skin tones or neutrals.

Avoid colors that blend with your skin tones and search for more contrast and compliment.

All the methods will very often lead you to the same conclusions. If you have a darker skin tone or a neutral, you can run the color gamut. So you're lucky, but you have to be cautious of the favorite colors for the other tones, such as navy's, blacks, and dark browns. These colors have less impact for a neutral or darker skin tone.

It is recommended that you spend a few minutes of research on the Internet to find a few methods and to select one that makes sense to you.

Many websites have great photos, illustrations, and easy guides to help you decide. Anyone can do it himself or herself at home, but experts abound if you require additional opinions. You can save yourself, and the environment, a lot of time and effort by knowing what will work best for you. You wont have to return as many items whose colors just don't work for you.

8

The Eighth Law

"There is no single outfit that is right for all occasions"

If you are hoping that you have one look that works in every occasion, you are wrong.

There is such a thing as being a fish out of water. For every circumstance there are clothes that suit it best. Having a synergy between the clothes and the instance shows thought, understanding, mastery, intent, and commitment. There are times when you need a few articles that can help you be prepared for any occasion.

Be a fish in water and dress for the part and the place.

When it comes to fashion, there are many sayings out there: "Dress for the position you want, not the position you have." "Don't out-dress the boss." You can out-dress the boss but don't out spend the boss. He or she knows what you earn and may hold you back for making too much. If you dress fabulous within your earning power you will be viewed as having amazing taste and style. That can be done on any budget without raising flags.

The fact is there is a correct look for each occasion and for each budget.

If you are going for an interview, you should dress for the position you desire. It is better to be overdressed than underdressed always. You may feel uneasy being overdressed, but you can take a few things off or loosen them up. Being underdressed is hard to overcome. Provided you know the occasion you should be able to use proper etiquette to ensure you look the best for it. Using your own style within these guidelines is what style is all about.

Being prepared and doing a little bit of research goes a long way.

You may notice this theme running through many of the laws. It has never been easier than it is today. Possessing great style is all about knowing the rules and norms. Have a good idea of the dress code for where you are going. Once you are familiar with what everyone else is going to do and expect, you can flip it. Style is in knowing how to bend the rules to a creative advantage. The style icon that bends the rules wins over one who merely plays it safe.

There are times when you may not have access to your full wardrobe, travel being one of those.

A few choice articles can get you through almost any situation without the need to rush to the store and purchase in haste. A good sport coat, trousers, and a white oxford shirt are great for male travelers. They are easily dressed up or down to suit the occasion. The little black dress is a no brainer for women, as it can do the same with varying accessories.

9

The Ninth Law

"Scent is the strongest memory maker"

If you want to be remembered, nothing will last as long as your scent.

How you smell will leave a lasting impression. Not just any impression, but one that can return a person to a memorable moment. This holds true if you smell good or bad. Some people know this and like to craft their body odor so you remember them—even if you want to vomit from the stench. Because you now know this, there are a few rules to help you craft your scent.

Think about how hard it is to leave a lasting impression.

Specifically, one that reaches back through the decades and returns you to a certain event. Scent is the strongest of the five senses for memory association. It has that unique ability to bring back visual images from the association. It is why Abercrombie and Fitch pump their scent through their stores and out into the mall. And it all happens unconsciously. So keep up your style. You'll want to be sure your positive image is great when the future brings in the past.

There are a few things to consider if using cologne, perfume, body spray or essential oils.

It should be noted that each of these reacts differently to a person's specific body chemistry. Essential oils are the strongest, most potent product, followed by perfume. Cologne and body sprays are diluted with alcohol. Alcohol opens the pores and speeds up the attachment, but it also speeds up the fade of the smell.

A scent is memorable if it is good or bad.

In fact, bad smell may be stronger, but you will

not want to remember it. It will leave a bad impression. After some time you become accustomed to a scent and tend to require more of it to smell it. Be careful not to overuse the scent; there can be too much of a good thing.

A few parting thoughts on crafting your own scent.

If you are using scented soap, shampoo, conditioner, and deodorant, the combination of different scents can all work against each other. In fact, it is difficult for them to work in unity. I suggest using as many scent-free toiletries as possible, or utilize a brand that bundles your favorite scent into these items. It is also wise not to share your secrets so your memory trigger isn't compromised with too many others utilizing your scent.

10

The Tenth Law

"Underwear is the foundation that your style is built upon"

If there is one topic that is always overplayed it is underwear and lingerie.

It is hard to find a witty interview with a celebrity where some snarky comment isn't made about their undergarments. People have widely different opinions on undergarments. There are views on how to wear them, which ones are appropriate, and whether to wear any at all. Whatever your outlook might be, your underwear, the condition of them, or lack of them, say plenty about you and your style.

We have become accustomed to seeing celebrities clad in underwear on billboards, buses, and magazines for decades.

Men and woman alike are showcased to get a rise out of us and grab our attention. It would be hard to imagine not giving significant thought to the bits of fabric that cover our most intimate of areas. Your choice of boxers, briefs, bikinis or boy-cuts, thongs, t-backs, or full cut panties, tell a lot about you. Every message you send to yourself reinforces your identity and style even if only to the most important person . . . YOU!

The type of underwear chosen is as broad as the opinions on those types.
We haven't even talked about fabrics such as silk, satin, cotton, nylon, and leather. Nothing brings out a vibrant dialogue like underwear, and who likes what or is wearing what. Discussion about this topic can become hot and passionate. It should be obvious why it is so important that your selection be right for the occasion. Even if that occasion calls for something secretly sexy, well especially if it calls for that. Be sure you're not caught ill prepared for that encounter.

How you wear them, what you wear, and where and when you wear them, can all be significant style "make or break" moments.

It goes without saying that if you choose ill-fitting under garments, the rest of your outfit (and probably your day) will not go so well. The optimum alignment here is that your inner style works with your outer style—which marries up to who you are as a person. That way, you are comfortable no matter what the occasion or situation.

Without a good foundation a structure cannot withstand storms when they arrive.

It is easy to skimp here. If you have been married or perma-single for any length of time this holds even more truth. If your garments are worn, pay it some mind and replace them.

These laws help us control things that can be controlled, so we can react calmly to the inevitable events that we cannot control. The underwear law is no different.

The 25 Indisputable Laws of Style

11

The Eleventh Law

*"A shoe can make or break
more than your outfit"*

The shoes make the man, and according to Marilyn Monroe, a girl in the right shoes can conquer the world.

It is a big world. Is there a right shoe for every occasion? There is! But if you are unsure of where to begin, I suggest the classics. They are a great place to start. Underwear may be the foundation garments, but the shoe supports the whole body. It is always a good idea to keep that in mind.

Would the prince still have fallen in love with Cinderella if she weren't wearing glass slippers?

Funny that clear heels are now often associated with strippers. Do shoes still make the man? According to many they do. Woman often judge a man by the shoes on his feet as much as they judge one another on shoe choice. The choice of footwear is paramount in the art of setting your style. The selection of one's footwear will speak volume's about whom they are, where they are, and where they want to go. Shoes are a great predictor of how they are going to get there. After all, they brought Dorothy back home.

Is there a right shoe for every occasion?

Have you ever been on a business interview wearing a suit and flip-flops? If you have, I'll wager you didn't get the position. Why are women permitted to show nearly bare feet at work and yet that would be unthinkable for a man? A woman in open-toed shoes can cause a riot in a prison, so they are forbidden there. What would happen if lumberjacks wore stilettos? How about running a marathon in high heels? Just as there is a right outfit for every occasion, there is also a right shoe (and hopefully a left one as well).

If you are not sure of the proper shoe etiquette, then start with the classics.

They got that way for a reason. Men do not have as wide a choice as women do. It is getting better, but still far behind. No man will be catching up to Imelda Marcos and her 3,000 pairs any time soon. The classics work. The men's wingtip brogues are as timeless as the stiletto. Fashion may dictate a chunky heel or wedge to be in style, but a male admirer will never frown on a stiletto.

The foot supports the entire body and a bad choice can hurt more than your image.

Good shoemakers make good shoes. Even sexy shoes can be comfortable from the right designer. The wrong footwear can result in your body overcompensating in other areas causing multiple issues in your posture and health. Luckily today many companies are designing footwear with technology built in so they can look good and still feel great. You can spend more for good shoes and enjoy the quality over a longer time.

12

The Twelfth Law

"Make accessories part of your style"

A great accessory can be the star of your outfit.

There are many rules and thoughts on accessories. It can be daunting on where to begin. A group of accessories may make up the majority of your look for the day. They can be the main attraction. Accessories can also be found guilty of stealing the show and your style. Is there such a thing as too much or too many? That depends, but there definitely can be too little.

A woman may find just the right accessory and be able to wear nothing but that.

Like a perfect pearl necklace and nothing else? If she goes out in public she may need to add a simple black dress or risk getting arrested. Accessories can be big, bold, and colorful. They may be small and demure. The key is to know that sometimes they are strong enough to carry the style without too much effort on the part of the other pieces.

A group of accessories can make your style as well.

Just look at Iris Apfel with her "here I am" look. She is brilliant, and her accessories are always put together in such an impactful, stylish way. I doubt that if she took Coco Chanel's advice on always removing one piece before you leave the house it would have a positive effect. On one hand, an icon that changed the world with costume jewelry; on the other, one who demonstrates iconic style with the use of all types of accessories. You can see what we mean by so many rules. Find what works for you.

That is not to say that accessories can't be found guilty of stealing the show from your style.

You want to obtain an impact as a whole and not be memorable piece by piece. In recent years, it has become fashionable again for the man to have a dandy appearance. He is seen sporting multiple colors and patterns with divine pocket squares, lapel pins, and the like. However, there is a time when the whole is not greater than the part and Coco's advice would heed well.

Can wearing too little have a negative impact?

Only if your beauty is so unfailing that any item of clothing at all would detract from your angelic style. I doubt many of us fall into that category, so lets accessorize and add cache and additional dimension to our style. Many a sales person is guilty of sizing up a client's prowess based on their watch or ring. Lets give them something to talk about.

#13

The Thirteenth Law

"Own Confidence"

Confidence–we envy those who have it, and pity those who don't.

Where does this marvelous quality come from? Are we born with it? Is it developed? Do we already have it? Don't be unsure, make a decision. It breeds confidence. In having your style pulled together, it boosts confidence. Do your research, it boosts confidence. Be yourself, there is no other you in the universe, have confidence in that. You are the best you because there is only you. A limited edition, or a one of a kind, is always worth more.

Confidence is our most attractive quality.

It is often valued more than money. Confidence is courage. It may not bring success but it will provide you the power to face any challenges along the path to get there. Once you make a decision on your style, you have to have an unwavering confidence in yourself. There is only one you, so be a confident you.

How do I get an unshakable confidence in myself?

Mark Twain suggests ignorance of everyone else's opinion but your own. Confidence is a muscle and the more you use it the more it develops. There is something majestic in believing so deep that it becomes real. In Man of La Mancha, Don Quixote believes without a doubt that he is a chivalrous knight. Is there anyone who did not see him exhibit those qualities? He lived it and became it through confidence.

Having your look pulled together is a natural confidence booster.

No matter how you feel, you are presenting yourself and your style with confidence. It is your armor; no one can take that away from you. Most people go through life just showing up, never trying, never developing. It's been said that eighty percent of the population falls into that category. If just showing up is a B student, how can you not have confidence? If you were trying harder, would it not result in a higher score?

Research builds knowledge and knowledge builds confidence.

Research how one should dress and what others have done; research the background of the person you are going to meet. Whatever your situation, a few minutes of research provides you with insight into a situation. That provides your mind with confidence that you can handle any question or issue that comes your way. If you wear it with confidence, you will portray confidence. A man can scare a bear away by showing confidence. Confidence is not the absence of fear; it is the ability to step past it. Owning confidence is everything in life!

14

The Fourteenth Law

"Don't sweat the socks"

To hose or not to hose is the question facing men and women alike today.

The bare leg for women and the bare ankle for men have taken on a life of their own. Hosiery is a great opportunity to add fun, wit, style, color, and class to your outfit. Just don't wear sweat socks with your suit—or your sandals for that matter. No one ever has uttered the words, "Your white sweat socks look great with those black shoes."

A few thoughts on when a bare leg or ankle beats a properly well attired hosiery choice.

If you are female and have gorgeous toned and tan legs you can pretty much get away with anything you want. If you fall marginally outside this level of leg superiority, you may want to sheer it up a bit. However, if your legs resemble a map or old wheat bread in any way, please cover them. No explanation should be necessary. Men, the same rules go for your ankles while wearing a suit, with one caveat: The average foot sweats an eight-ounce glass of water a day, and leather is not a friend of water.

Hosiery is such a fun way to add color and texture to your style.

A fun, bright pop of color for a man can draw the eye to that amazing shoe choice. Hosiery can add whimsy and wit to somber business attire in a subtle way. Ladies, the amount of amazing hosiery and nylon options available to you is infinite. The ability to add sheen, shine, matte, color, texture, and pattern is limitless. There are many qualities and deniers for different climates. If you haven't found something you like, maybe you haven't looked far enough.

Don't wear socks with sandals.

That goes for both men and woman, and includes monks as well. If you are an athlete and you're in transition at the gym from playing gear, then it's acceptable. The sliders and socks look works for you. Other than that, it is no-go. It doesn't say, "I'm comfortable," it says "I'm lazy." Wearing sweat socks with a suit makes the statement that you can't afford dress socks. Maybe pizza delivery boy is a better position for you. Now take that suit off, you're embarrassing yourself.

If it comes with garters, It's great!

There is a reason that at every wedding I have ever attended the groom slowly removes a garter from his new wife's leg and tosses it to the bachelors. It is because garter belts, garters, and stockings are sexy. I can't speak for the male sock garters on each leg to hold up the dress socks, but rumor has it they are too.

15

The Fifteenth Law

"You can leave your hat on"

Hats can add great panache to one's style.

Hats have attitude. Some people are known simply by their hats. There are so many choices when it comes to a hat. Some hats are for function and should not be considered for fashion or style, but merely for protection. There are times when you should leave your hat on and other times when you should absolutely take it off.

Hats have attitude and sometimes you just feel like wearing a different hat.

We have passed the time when everyone donned hats. Hats were worn out of necessity when the industrial revolution produced so much soot in the cities that wearing a hat was necessary. It is said that President John F. Kennedy ruined the hat business for men, when as a young president he would appear without one. Imagine that! Just before that moment in time, men and woman always wore hats.

Some people are known for their hats, or by their hats.

I can't imagine Slash without his top hat, Winston Churchill either. I tend to picture Humphrey Bogart with his on. It seems Samuel L. Jackson tends to favor a hat. A woman can look fabulous in a hat. Marlene Dietrich is a notorious hat wearer, as is the Queen of England. I believe Lady Gaga is as well. I remember my mother use to wear big brimmed floppy hats in the seventies. Some guys wear ski hats in Florida at the gym! A hat gives you such style that sometimes what seems odd or out of place becomes cool.

Some hats are purely for function.

You may not look too cool running around with

a firefighter's heavy hat on, but then again someone might just be able to pull it off. Hard hats are functional so workers don't get hit in the head by falling debris at the work site. That didn't stop every member of Village People from wearing hats. Some hats are meant only to keep the suns rays from burning our heads and faces. Still, even a hat with that sort of function can be stylish

There are times when you should take your hat off.

It is a sign of respect for the male to remove his hat during the national anthem. He is also expected not to wear his hat in church in some religions. It use to be that men were expected not to wear a hat indoors, but that doesn't seem to follow anymore. For women, anything goes. They can wear their hat all the time. No need to take it off. A hat can make a woman look stylish, even sexy. I once dated a woman just because of her hat. A tiny miniature hat it was. Well it's what attracted me to her anyway. She had such style. In the words of Joe Cocker: "You can leave your hat on."

The 25 Indisputable Laws of Style

16

The Sixteenth Law

"Contrast creates interest"

Thoughtful, planned opposition can create balance.

Monochromatic can look great, but contrast creates interest and excitement. The juxtaposition need not be just plain black and white. Using the color spectrum creates vibrancy. Contrast draws the eye, calling attention to a focal point of interest. It makes the observer stop and think—and it makes you more interesting.

Juxtaposition is why a man's dress tuxedo is black and white.

The boldness of the black suit creates a sharp contrast to the white shirt. This draws all the attention to a man's face. To add interest, the lapel and jetted pockets are satin, creating an additional contrast in texture. This provides added dimension and appeal but leaves the juxtaposing and facial framing the main focal point.

Polychromatic dressing can be quite powerful.

The addition of a contrasting or complimenting color can completely elevate a look. It also can add a new dynamic that creates depth to the style. It can be achieved through the use of colored accessories as well. But be careful, having too much going on creates a clown car effect. Where we expect more and more to just keep happening, it may be entertaining, but is not very stylish.

Think about where you want to draw the eye.

It is wisest to highlight your best assets. Not sure which is your strength? Have people routinely complimented you on a particular feature? You can start there or ask a friend. Maybe your eyes are your best asset? Why not highlight them by selecting an accessory that really pulls out the color? If your cleavage is your best asset and you highlight it, don't be upset if the twins draw all the attention

Constructing contrast creates excitement. Remember, judgment is passed in the first four seconds. In developing style you want to be memorable in a positive light. Adding depth through contrast and conflict creates interest. This extends the four seconds, making a deeper impression.

17

The Seventeenth Law

*"If you want to be interesting,
be interested in others"*

It is said that the sweetest sound in the world is one's own name.

People desire to feel like they have meaning. They will like you, and associate with you, even if they speak the entire conversation. If you learn to ask insightful questions, it is possible to keep a discussion moving just by adding a quip or two. The perception of a good conversationalist is built on listening. If you want to be remembered as an interesting person, and not a shallow shell, you have to be interested in others.

We all have egos and some of us are more aware of this than others.

When a person is remembered it makes them feel relevant. "Hey there, you" is not a great greeting. If you use the person's name when addressing them, it will help you remember it. You can also make a little rhyme that helps you remember.

When we are genuinely interested in what is going on with others, it makes for good conversation.

This is preferable over one-sided banter where it is all "let me tell you more about me." If you have the opportunity to either talk about yourself or engage the other person and ask about them, choose the latter. They will be sure to find you more interesting than if you told them all about how wonderful you are.

It is not hard to develop this good habit.

All you have to do is learn to ask questions. Don't ask like a probing mother, which is just annoying. Try not to ask the usual questions either, like, "What do you do?" Pick out something that you can be interested in. If you are in their house, maybe you can ask about an interesting picture or knick-knack. If you just met, maybe you can ask about her earrings or broach? Ask the person where he or she bought it. Do they like that store? This helps start a conversation. Most people are thankful to be speaking about something they know rather than trying to feign interest about something they know nothing about.

Having style and being an interesting person go hand in hand.

Memorable people are forgiven for all sorts of eccentricities if they are interesting. Interesting people get invited to parties. Why? Because the host knows that it is quid pro quo with interesting people. They know their other guests will get to mingle, and vice versa. Great looking wallflowers are as exciting as watching paint dry. They don't get invited; they stay home with the wallpaper.

18

The Eighteenth Law

"Style is cultivated like a garden"

Creating a style is like cultivating a garden.

You must weed out bad things, trim, prune, water, and then bloom. Having style is not a "set it and forget it" formula. It takes time to cultivate and grow in order to blossom. You can change your look today and in a day. If you want to establish a style, it takes time. Your style should grow like a garden. You add new plants as your eye and tastes change and develop.

Crafting a style, developing it, and nurturing it, means that it lives and grows.

That is what keeps it interesting and out of the "fad" bin. Your wardrobe, library, and friends should all grow. Sometimes they get too unruly and need to be trimmed back and refocused. It is best to make this continual. That way you can avoid a massive cut back where all your branches look chopped and bare for a time.

It is not a "set it and forget it" formula.

That is what happens to gardens that are not tended. They get overgrown and are eventually changed entirely. That may sound good to you but it is not, and it is an ugly process. It is much better to work on it, build it, maintain it, add to it, and remove from it, but the essence stays the same.

It takes time to develop style.

If you change drastically in a day your environment and friends will not understand and think you are going through some sort of . . . something. When you make style part of your life and part of who you are, it is a lifelong commitment. It is not a job, it is your life. You have to have fun with it. Grow and develop.

You will not fit into the same clothes that you did fifteen years ago. That's both physically and stylistically unlikely.

Your tastes change as the world moves on.

You will adopt new hobbies, read new books, and maybe even live in different places. These experiences change you. It is expected that your style be flexible and change with you. Your style should be developing and growing along with your life to reflect your life. Cultivated and curated to be uniquely yours.

19

The Nineteenth Law

"Being trendy is a show not a style"

Any fool can blindly adopt a fad or a trend.

It does not mean you have style. However, it does call into question your taste. Trends have a short shelf life. They are disposable. You can have some laughs but don't mistake entertainment for style. That's not to say you should be ignorant of trends in your style— such as updates to fit and details.

The trendy quickly becomes tacky.

We say, "blindly adopting a trend" because what people follow blindly usually turns out to be a bad idea. If it did not start there in the first place, it certainly will end up there. Being trendy is shortsighted and has limited depth. If you want to be trendy, go into a cheap shop and buy what's on the mannequin. BAM! Now you're trendy. But, that sounds like the low end of the pool, and too shallow to be meaningful for long.

There is a sucker born every minute, just don't be one of them.

Did you adopt the snuggy trend? How about wearing your jeans with the waist below your ass? Is Ashton Kutcher still rolling in his Trucker hat? Maybe you felt Ed Hardy artwork was great before it was plastered all over everything? Did you get an Ed Hardy tattoo?

Its fun to have some laughs and give a gag gift or two.

But you really don't want this to be your signature style. Everyone has fun with the new thing or hot new "must have" item. Be selective and don't waste your money on trends and fads. You can watch them on television and check them out on the Internet. Enjoy being entertained, but don't mistake it for style. Don't buy into somebody selling fast style. The "just add water" philosophy is not right for you or your dignity.

Trends in style are a completely different thing.

These are movements and changes in hemlines, details, seasonal color combinations, shoes, and heel heights, among other things. As a person of style you should know a lot about these changes. You should keep yourself abreast of these alterations even if you choose not to adopt them into your style for personal reasons. Style is all about knowing yourself and knowing what's going on, then mastering the two of those into your custom crafted look.

20

The Twentieth Law

"Repetition is reputation"

It takes time and consistency to cement your personal style.

Your reputation is built one day upon the next. You can make an immediate impact, but repetition will build your reputation. You are what you think, and you're known for what you do. Being consistent makes your reputation solid. It becomes who you are.

There is a reason we call it developing a style and not adopting a style.

You adopt a trend and you develop a style. Trends change constantly and so your look changes constantly. Style is built day upon day of showcasing taste and panache. So much so that when someone begins to imitate your look, people will reference that they look like you. This does not mean wearing the same costume day after day. That is consistent but not stylish.

If you were to showcase your style today, it will have an immediate impact.

It takes consistency for that impact to build into reputation. In a world of relentless media coverage, we are bombarded with images from the time we wake up until the time we go to sleep. The truly impactful style images are the ones that get saved and remembered. Think of your style as a blog where you post an influential or inspirational style shot every day. You want the images to have consistency in theme but avoid redundancy.

It is said that we are what we think about.

Our dominant thoughts shape our outer selves. We are remembered for what we do, or don't do. There is no easier way to develop great thinking and style than by doing what you say you will do. In essence, keeping your word builds style and reputation. People remember people who do what they say they are going to do, especially in a world where that happens less and less.

If you are consistent in your actions this will build your reputation.

Often people lament that others should be remembered for their best selves, or for whom they would like to be. Life is simple. You are remembered for what you do, period. You can always improvo, change, and adapt. It just requires that you build enough consistency in the new actions so they override past memories. Constant repetition of great values and style will build your reputation.

21

The Twenty-First Law

"A smile can make someone's day, especially your own"

The best accessory to any outfit is your smile.

You should put it on first thing in the morning when you look in the mirror. Smiles are contagious and they make other people smile. They may also make other people wonder what you are up to. Smiles are attractive and release chemicals that make you feel better. A smile uses fewer muscles than a frown. A smile can change a person.

People like happy people.

A smile is the universal language that says, "Hello, I am approachable." Eventually, we should all realize that we are in sales. We are selling ourselves—even to ourselves—all the time. Putting on a smile is an easy way to fake it until you make it. As soon as you start smiling, you start feeling better, and so does everyone around you.

Smiles are very contagious.

If a person who is smiling looks at you, it is hard to not smile back. It has been said that happiness is grin deep. When you smile it will put you, and others, at ease. You become not just approachable, but attractive. Like attracts like. No one wants to be around a person that is vexatious to the spirit. A frowner is a downer. A smile-ler is an extra mile-ler.

When you smile, it sends a positive message to the brain.

This in turn releases endorphin's that immediately make you feel better. It is hard to believe it can be that easy, but it's true. The saying "it takes fewer muscles to smile than it does to frown," has been around for so long that it has become folklore. Folklore often has some truth to its reasoning even if it hasn't been proven as fact. Smile. It is a free, happy drug that makes you look younger.

A smile changes people in a positive way.

A smile can even be used defensively. If someone is giving you a hard time, just keep smiling and it will really drive him or her nuts. A smile can lighten a mood or a situation. It is contagious. A smile can even make strangers smile back at you. Smiles are free, so using a smile will not only make your day, but will undoubtedly make someone else's day too.

22

The Twenty-Second Law

"Be passionate about something"

It is important that you develop a hobby or find something that you are passionate about. Develop a compelling enthusiasm; something that you can hold an in-depth conversation about. Make it the one thing that your friends would say describes who you are. Having passion about something, not someone, adds depth to your character. Be careful, because passion can be a two-sided blade that cuts both ways.

Passion is having a compelling interest or aspiration for something.

Have a hobby, sport, cause, or study that you know a lot about. It can be anything: fashion, photography, finance, health, fitness, music, etc. A person's persona changes when they are speaking about a thing they are passionate about. You can tell they are engaged in the subject and their intensity arouses more interest from the listener.

If you are not sure what you are passionate about then ask your friends.

What is the one thing that they would list when describing who you are? Does that one dominating thing align with your vision of who you are? If it does not, then you have some work to do. If your friends list work as your most passionate pursuit then that is likely what you talk about most. If you love your work, that's fine. But, if it is not your true passion, then this area needs development. You need to find your real passion.

When you have a passion for something, you can talk about it with ease.

Having something you are excited about can add depth to your character. People are attracted to your level of enthusiasm because it places value on that which you are passionate about. Something of little value now grows with more importance when you add in your passion for the subject. You can throw yourself into a discussion and insert meaningful insights into the conversation.

You should always be seeking to grow and acquire knowledge in your chosen field of endeavor.

This is reflected in your style. You become committed to a passion and have more dimensions to your personality. Be careful because passions burn brightly and can become all-consuming obsessions. You do not want to neglect family and friends and become reclusive with your passion. You want it to burn brightly and be a light of interest when and where you show it.

23

The Twenty-Third Law

"Be mysterious, not secret"

Being mysterious is sexy and intriguing.

Being secretive tends to make you look like you have something to hide. Mystery creates wonder. It is attractive and stimulating, adding complexity to your style. Being secretive is a turn off and casts suspicion upon your character. With mystery, the less you reveal, the more people wonder. Generating this wonder is a chief aim of style.

Being mysterious can be as simple as smiling.

People will wonder, "Why is he or she smiling?" "What are they so happy about?" "Did they just win the lottery or get a promotion at work?" "What does the person smiling know that I don't know that is making them smile?" "Why won't they tell me what perfume or cologne they use?" Because mystery creates curiosity and intrigue, that's why.

Mystery adds depth by coaxing others into wanting to know more about you.

It makes you thought provoking. These very simple ideas, a smile, a refusal to reveal knowledge, can be employed with great effect. When you craft a style with complexity, you have to have layers that can be peeled back, always revealing more, but never revealing all.

Being secret is a different story altogether.

Secretiveness causes suspicion. It may be close to mysteriousness, but is perceived negatively. Secretive is a defensive posture that works at hidden aims. What are those aims, and are they directed at me, or will they be used against me? It creates a feeling in others of wanting to put distance between you and them. It destroys a sense of style instead of igniting it.

Mystery is operating in an air of beauty, awe, intrigue, and wonder.

Intrigue makes you want to discover and know more. A deep desire to understand and get to know the person is created. It will make them wonder, why are you so mysterious? It is playful and makes one want to get close; to understand and uncover. It pulls people in as you reveal a little more . . . and a little more.

24

The Twenty-Fourth Law

"Style is more important than substance, initially"

This may be hard to accept, or easy to accept, depending on your personality.

The truth is that you are most judged, weighed, and measured during the time you set your first impression. That impression is generally made within four seconds of someone looking at you. That is not sufficient time for you to prove your substance. If you fail to realize the importance of style to get you past that initial assessment, it is almost impossible to change that first impression.

It will take a very long time to alter that first impression once it is set.

During a first impression, visual cues will fill in blanks on a pre-written form in the memory of the person on whom you are imprinting that impression. First impressions are generally formed through intuition and gut instinct from past data collected. Most people struggle with changing their first impressions of someone because it calls into question their own ability to assess.

More often than not a first impression doesn't change.

Let us compare two people. One who has substance but lacks style, and one with style who lacks substance. It will take a long time for the observer to discover who really has the substance. In short, the person with style will fare better at first impressions. That person also will have the luxury of time on their side. It will take successive interactions to recast a first impression and reset it. It may take considerable time before an opportunity surfaces to showcase any substance.

Ignore your style and others may ignore your substance.

The "style is more important than substance, initially" law must be seriously considered.

Every effort must be taken to position your style to support and align with your personal goals; especially when considering who you want to be and how you want to be remembered. If your style and substance are aligned, the full "you" is positioned for maximum exposure. Your self-presentation will be much stronger than someone lacking either one or the other.

Today we live in a world that has multiple platforms for making impressions and setting them.

We live in a culture obsessed with image. Consider selfies and social media. You can see how much a first impression is developed today prior to a face-to-face meeting. If you follow the 25 laws of indisputable style, you can master both style and substance. You can live without fear of casting a poor impression. You can showcase what you are really about.

25

The Twenty-fifth Law

"It is better to be overdressed than underdressed"

It is difficult to think of a situation where being overdressed isn't preferable to being underdressed.

You can always loosen up a bit and remove a few items. If you are underdressed, it is very hard to meet the expectations of code unless you can run out and shop. That is not likely. There is proper attire for every occasion. It is possible to be outfitted entirely incorrectly. That situation is not being overdressed, that is being out of place.

If you are overdressed for a meeting, you can always take off a tie and jacket.

You can loosen up a bit; hell you can even take off your socks if no one has seen you yet. It is still preferable to be the best-dressed person in the room. Better to risk a look of being well put together than to risk looking like you don't care. When you develop style, your look becomes an expectation.

There is appropriate attire for every occasion.

You would not wear a three-piece suit or skirt to go mountain climbing. Swim trunks are out of place in the snow, just as swimming in a pea coat is not appropriate. If you are going hunting, it is wise to know what crowd you will be with. Is it the Orvis and Beretta expectations of Fifth Avenue? Or are you going with the Cabella's and Dick's Sporting Goods group? Both can outfit you for hunting but with very different results of style.

It is possible to be outfitted incorrectly.

Just ask anyone who has gone dressed to a costume party to discover there is no costume party. That would be very uncomfortable indeed! But we are talking about being overdressed versus underdressed. This is a matter of understanding more about the right looks for the occasion. Jeans at a wedding are probably going to fall into the underdressed category. Wearing a tux at a beach wedding, where the groom is in shorts and a Hawaiian shirt, would still be preferable than the other way around.

Oscar Wilde said that you can never be over-dressed or over-educated.

The people that would disagree with Mr. Wilde probably would not read this book. You, on the other hand, did read it. Because of this, I will guess that you agree with him and the twenty-fifth law. Being overdressed is not really an issue if you are confident in the way you look. You look better than everyone else. You are garnering a lot of attention. Isn't that the whole point of being able to master style anyway?

#26

The Secret Law

"Do not become prisoner to an image you create"

How do you become prisoner of the image you have crafted?

When you have sufficiently developed your style, you are now recognizable as a style icon. Your friends, coworkers, peers, and family— maybe even a few circles of influence further than that—think of you this way. You have crafted a look and that look is your personal brand.

Don't be afraid to change or showcase your patented look for fear that people won't know you.

Now you have to be careful not to become a prisoner of that image. Maybe you fear that you will stop getting preferential treatment at the hottest clubs and restaurants. Fear is a style killer.

Many people have gotten stuck with a

look that was very successful for them.

They were so successful at developing a style they had followers and imitators. If they changed, they risked losing the following they had. That following wants what it wants. Think of the many famous people who must continue to wear their image for fear of not being noticed. The same look day in and day out. That sounds like a prison to me.

Many a rock star would go unnoticed if they did not continue to wear their defining look.

Over the years we have seen many aged rockers go back to their old image to sell more records, books, and tour tickets. Some entertainers have transcended this prison. Madonna is one of them. Madonna rebranded herself with each new album. She has continued to adapt, grow, and evolve. She has remained interesting through her career and is not a prisoner to just one look or style

Style should have depth and adaptation so that it continues to remain interesting. Keep your style evolving. That is the goal. Keep it moving and growing so people want to see what you will do next. Avoid the trap of having only one successful look.

"Have a style budget for maximum impact"

Mastering style is quite an endeavor.

That is why most people have not done it. Now that you're familiar with the 25 indisputable laws of style, you are better prepared to make the next impression a lasting one. Ask yourself, honestly, how many of the laws do you employ today? Imagine the impact on your life when you begin to utilize even just a few more. Many of them are free. Here is a formula to plan purchases on the ones that are not.

How do you stretch your style budget to have maximum impact?

This is one of the best tips I can share with you. I call it the "use-per-dollar equation." First determine how often you can use any item you are thinking of purchasing. Make sure you consider longevity as well. Socks are not going to last as long as a watch. Separate items with long-term usability from those with limited use. Don't make high-dollar purchases on limited-use items.

Big-ticket expenditures work like this:- Shoes, belts, coats, bags, and watches are items *you can use every single day*. Therefore, you can buy the very best and spend more. The number of uses goes up dramatically and this brings the cost-per-use down drastically.

Let's break it down:
A limited-use purchase is an item that you can use maximum once per week. A new shirt has a higher cost-per-use. A shirt worn once per week will wear out in less than a year. The average testing for apparel companies goes to 20 home launderings, so 50 is stretching it a bit. A heavy-use purchase is an item like a new coat or bag. It can be used every day.

Formula: (Price/days of use = cost-per-use)

Example:

Bag $1500.00 / 365 = $4.10 per use over one year.

(Each additional use time lowers the per-use cost.)

Shirt $300.00 / 50 = $6.00 per wear over one year.

(A shirt will look pretty worn before 50 uses.)

You are getting more bang for your buck, and more purchasing power, on items used more often. A new expensive bag costs less per use than a new expensive shirt. An additional benefit: Buying better products you'll use every day elevates your style. Tom Ford shoes, belt, and bag will look and feel much more pulled together than purchasing random high-ticket items that are not used as frequently. Those random purchases make you feel like you spent too much. A style budget can help you maximize your wardrobe while making intelligent decisions.

Sean Coyle is a creative leader with a visionary talent and savvy business acumen. Throughout his career Sean has been sought out by leading global apparel companies to imagine, create, and develop, new brands & product lines. He is a catalyst for positive change in design, building and leading tight creative teams where the output per associate significantly lowers operating expense; contributing positive sales growth and providing market magic.

Sean Coyle

The 25 Indisputable Laws of Style